Sarah Bed

Forty Nights

Essay by Margaret Iversen

Sarah Beddington,
New York, 2000

Vision and Blindness

I approach the painting in a gallery and see… what? A field of interference. A screen or veil woven of fine strands of paint. The veil's threads scintillate and shimmer creating a dazzling optical effect. Shifting my position so that I am directly opposite the painting, a strange interior scene materializes behind the screen. It is a semi-public anonymous space like a restaurant or hotel lobby, but deserted. The fluorescent strip lighting is artificial, as are the potted plants that vainly strive to enliven this everyday limbo. I strain to see into the space, trying to fathom its depths, but as I shift position, the image is once again engulfed by darkness.

Sarah Beddington has created a technique for evoking an experience familiar to us all. The scene that looms up and disappears has the strangeness and evanescence of a dream scene, which scrutiny also obliterates. The type of interior space she depicts is a *mise-en-scène* for some kind of encounter, whether good or bad, provoking both desire and dread, promising pleasure and danger. The oscillation between screen and scene re-enforces this ambivalence on a formal level, intercepting the visible with the invisible, crossing vision with blindness.

The spectator's unsettling experience of finding and losing the image, recapitulates the artist's procedure. Beddington trawls the city looking for interior spaces that have a modern haunted look. She takes a photograph and reproduces it in paint, sometimes creating a blurred, unfocused effect. When the painting is dry, she covers it with another layer of paint. She then scores fine vertical lines through the still tacky surface, partially revealing the image beneath. It is a delicate operation that sometimes results in her literally losing the image.

I can think of one artist with a comparable artistic procedure. Gerhard Richter also works the fascinating interface between photography and painting, and both conceive of that interface as the very inverse of a 'photo-realist' aesthetic. What we see in their work is not so much a representation of something as a presentation of an absence. It is significant, then, that their procedures involve a moment of (threatened) destruction. Richter uses a squeegee pulled across tacky paint to create his smeared abstractions and scratches the surface of his painted images derived from photographs to create a blurred effect. Richter's smearing and scratching and Beddington's scored screen make their paintings border on both figuration and abstraction in a way which declares that, although their paintings may be figurative, the point of them is not to be found in any correspondence with some phenomenal reality. Rather, both artists aim to touch the real.

The real is the term given by the psychoanalyst, Jacques Lacan, to what must be thrust aside in order for me to live – to establish a coherent identity and a consistent world. Yet, the real sometimes returns, troubling the clear water of that world, stirring up clouds of enigma and causing anxiety. One should not be surprised to find photography allied with the artistic ambition to touch the real. Think of the Surrealists' harnessing of the camera's blind mechanism in their quest to find an unconscious reality that would unsettle our false, complacent reality. Or, recall Roland Barthes' discussion in *Camera Lucida* of the wounding 'punctum' of certain photographs.

Barthes sometimes refers to the punctum as a little spot (*petit tâche*) or stain, making an oblique reference to Lacan's famous discussion of Holbein's *The Ambassadors*. That discussion centred on the obscure, oblong object floating in the foreground of the painting. This is the stuff that is necessarily extruded from the consistent world of the Ambassadors. Leaving the gallery and glancing sidelong at the painting, Lacan finds that the anamorphic smudge has resolved into a death's head, an avatar of the real. The experience he describes resonates with that of viewing Beddington's paintings, except that an oblique view of one of her paintings abruptly brings the shutters down on the depicted scene. It is a non-figurative brush with death.

Lacan's account of *The Ambassadors* contrasts the composed world of the depiction with the incomprehensible stain. In Beddington's work, the depicted scene also invokes desire and loss. A comparison with another painter, Edward Hopper, is helpful in thinking about her imagery. *Automat* (1927) shows a young woman sitting in an otherwise empty restaurant at night. We can't fathom her thoughts, but behind her is a large window in which we see nothing but darkness and the reflection of two rows of ceiling lights in steep perspectival recession. The lights have a vertiginous lure. Beddington's paintings turn this scene inside out. Instead of the metaphorical black window, she intercepts our view with the dark screen. Instead of depicting a lone figure peering into her coffee cup, the spectator is left peering into a strangely familiar space.

The scenes in Beddington's work are like up-dated Hopper spaces, but without the figures. In their use of 'photographic' framing and cropping, both Hopper and Beddington produce scenes that stress their partial, contingent nature. They also have the quality of film-stills in which narrative is suspended. Beddington underscores this quality by producing series of pictures that zoom in or circle around a space. The effect of the composition is to make the trajectory of the image aim outside the frame, creating a 'blind field'. Beddington further amplifies this effect with closed doors, or partial views into adjoining rooms. These blind fields kindle the desire of the spectator to see, as does the painted screen. There is also a temporal blind field at work: the empty spaces are the *mise-en-scène* for some encounter for which we are either too early or too late.

Beddington's recent work, *Forty Nights*, pushes the analogy with cinema to an extreme. It consists of forty small images, fragments forming what she calls 'a not-quite narrative'. Here we have a distinct sense of slowly moving through a labyrinthine space, picking our way along corridors and up stairs. Perhaps because the framing is so tight, the colours so intense and the subjects so banal, the feeling of scanning the space for something that cannot be seen becomes intense. Do we seek, like a detective, clues to solve a mystery? Or search for traces that would remind us of what happened in these rooms? All we can be sure of is the truth of the phrase that sums up Lacan's theory of vision and desire: 'What I look at is never what I want to see'.

Margaret Iversen

Forty Nights

 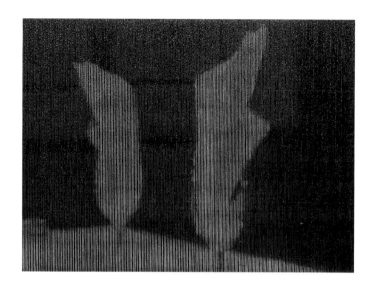

 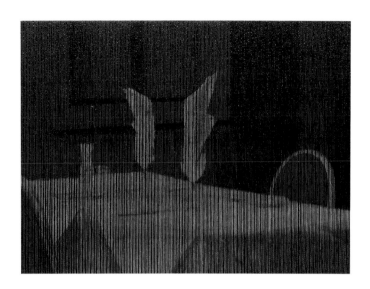

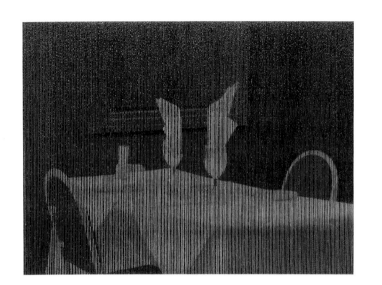

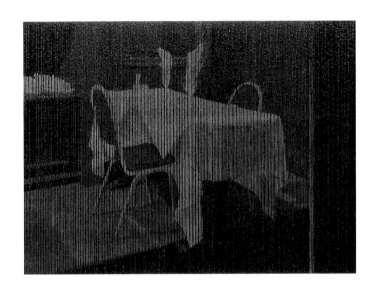

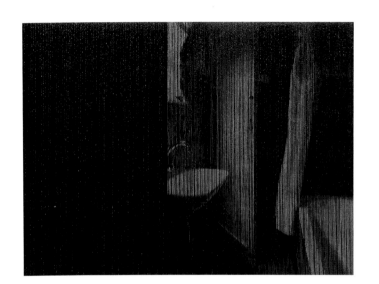 

 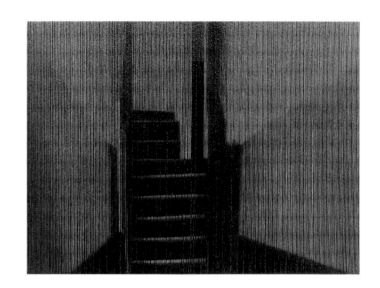

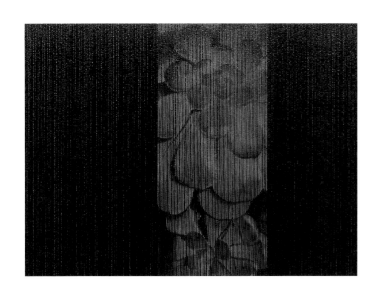

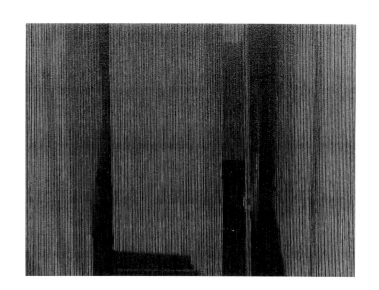

 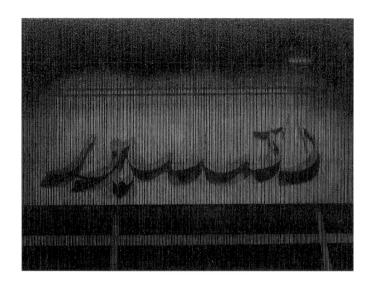

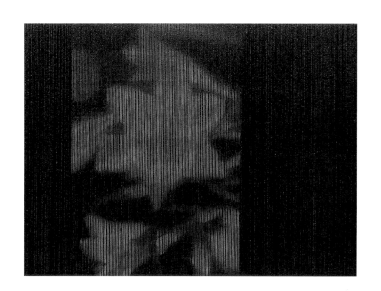
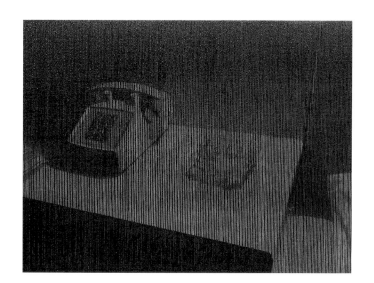

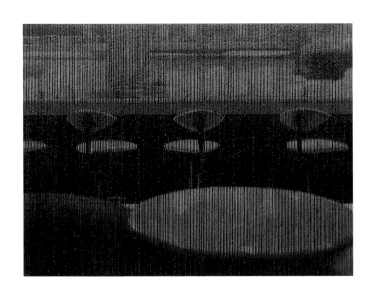 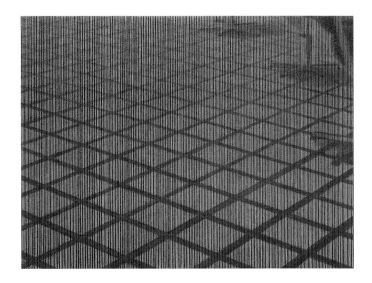

 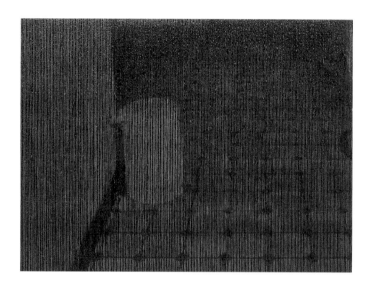

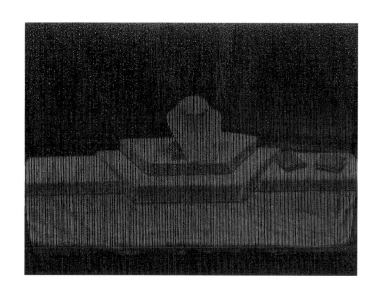 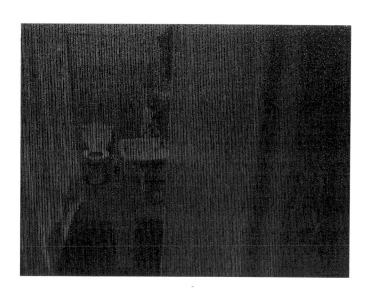

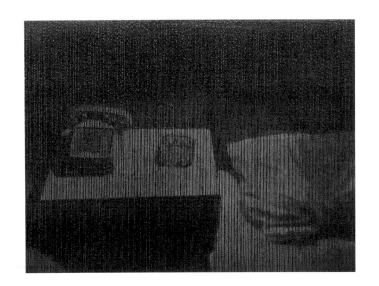 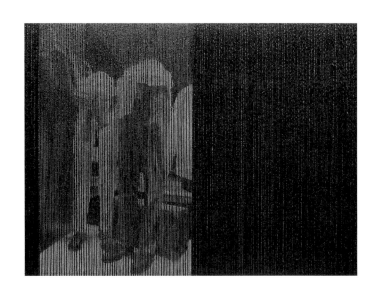

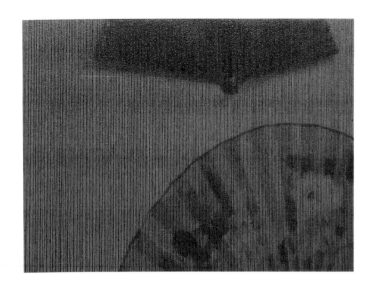

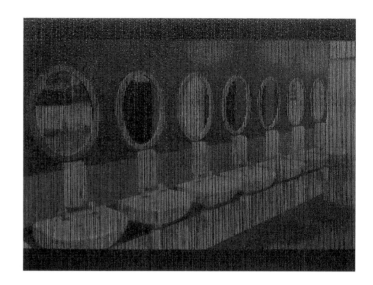

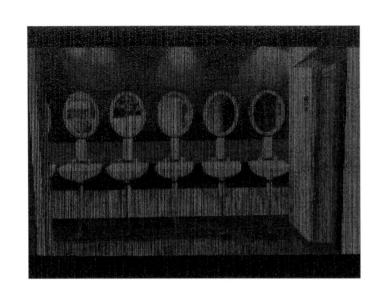

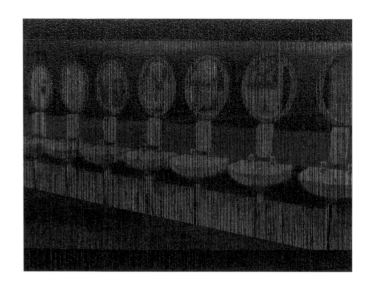

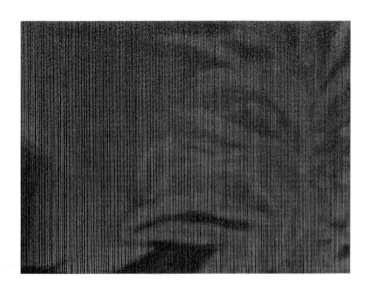

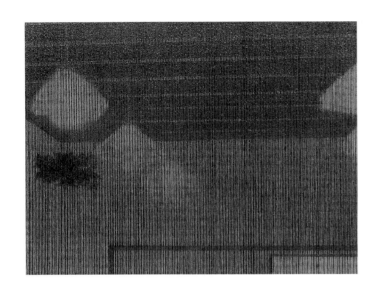

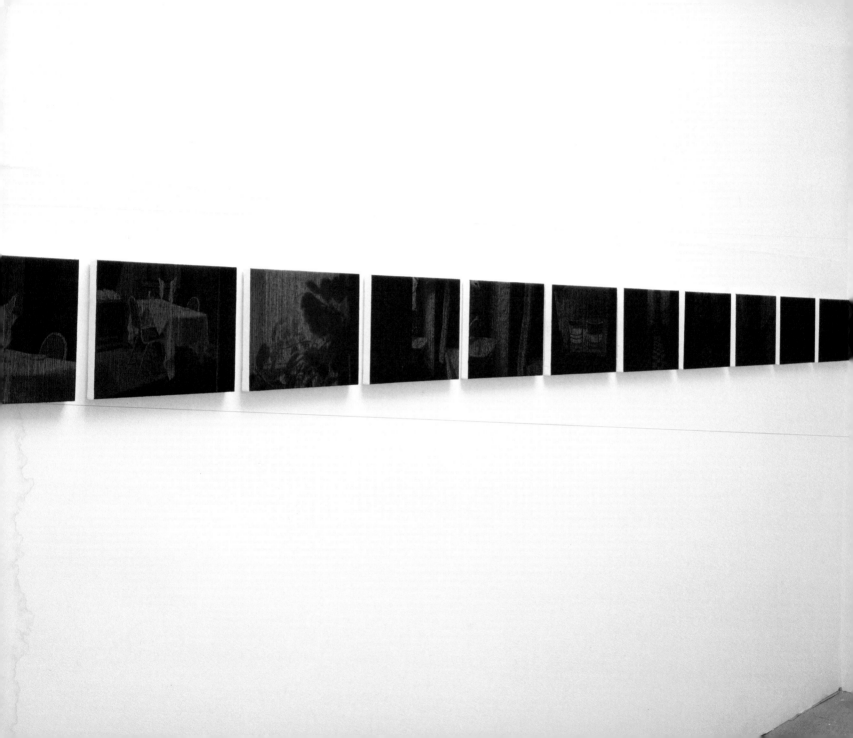

Biography

Solo Exhibitions

1964
Born in Wiltshire

1990 – 93
City and Guilds of London Art School

1994 – 96
MA Fine Art at Central St Martins College
of Art & Design

Lives and works in London

June 2001
Hales Gallery, London

November 1999
Galleri Wallner, Malmö, Sweden

January 1999
Hales Gallery, London

Forty Nights: forty canvases, oil on canvas, 2001
each canvas 25.5 × 34.5 cm (10 × 13½ ins)

Selected Group Exhibitions

2000
'Not Enough', Velan Centro d'Arte
Contemporanea, Turin

'The Wreck of Hope', the Nunnery Gallery, London

'Introduction Service', Zwemmer Gallery, London

1999
'Bankside Browser', Tate Modern project, London

NatWest Art Prize, Lothbury Gallery, London

'Versus V', Carignano, Turin

John Moores 21, Walker Art Gallery, Liverpool

1998
Whitechapel Open, Whitechapel Art Gallery,
London

Towner Art Gallery, Eastbourne

1997
'Switch It Off', Kyoto, Japan

Hales Gallery, London

'History', The Mag Collection, Ferens Art
Gallery, Hull

1996
Whitechapel Open, Whitechapel Art Gallery,
London

'Directions', Lethaby Gallery, London

Selected Bibliography

Tan, Eugene: 'Sarah Beddington', ArtReview, Volume L1V, June 2001

Kyander, Pontus: 'As if Looking Through a Venetian Blind', Sydsvenskan, December 13, 1999

Klinthage, Jörgen: 'Conscious Quotes and Melancholy Urban Spaces', Arbetet, December 13, 1999

John Moores 21(catalogue), p.38, Walker Art Gallery, Liverpool, 1999

Versus V (catalogue), Ex Lanificio Bona, Carignano, Italy

Barbieri, Annalisa: 'Isn't a Camera Enough?', Independent on Sunday, Culture, June 20, 1999

Marlow, Tim: NatWest Art Prize 1999 (catalogue), p.9, Lothbury Gallery, London

Mullins, Charlotte: 'Suited and Muted', The Independent on Sunday, Culture, May 16, 1999

Burton, Jane: 'Wall-to-Wall Talent', Sunday Times, Metro, April 24 – 30, 1999

Exley, Roy: 'Sarah Beddington: Hales Gallery', zingmagazine, pp.210 – 212, spring/summer 1999

Dyer, Richard: 'Sarah Beddington', Time Out, p.49, February 3 – 10 1999

Von Planta, Regina: 'Sarah Beddington at Hales Gallery', Kunst Bulletin, pp.42 – 43, January/ February 1999

Fulcher, Dawn: 'Sarah Beddington', Contemporary Visual Arts, Issue 21, p.88, December 1998 – February 1999

Greenan, Althea: 'Is History His or Hers?', Make, No.82, p.24, December 1998 – February 1999

Benjamin, Marina: 'Whitechapel Open: No beef,… just a pack of jokers', Evening Standard, April 9, 1998

'History', The Mag Collection (catalogue), p.25, Ferens Art Gallery, Hull, 1997

This catalogue has been produced in association with Hales Gallery to coincide with the show 'Forty Nights'

2 June – 7 July 2001 at Hales Gallery, London

Margaret Iversen is Professor of Art History and Theory at the University of Essex. Her publications concerning the themes of 'Vision and Blindness' are 'What is a Photograph?', Art History, 17:3, September 1994, pp.450 – 463 and 'In the Blind Field: Hopper and the Uncanny', Art History, 21:3, September 1998, pp.409 – 429

All photography by Peter White / FXP

Designed by Herman Lelie
Typeset by Tristan de Lancey
Printed by PJ Print, London

Hales Gallery
70 Deptford High Street
London SE8 4RT
telephone: +44 (0)20 8694 1194
fax: +44 (0)20 8692 0471
e-mail: halesgallery@btinternet.com

ISBN 1 870 282 27 2